FROM THE
AMERICA'S 20
FAVORITE SERIES

AMERICA'S
200

FAVORITE
PRAISE CHORUSES
&
HYMNS

Compiled by Ed Kee
Edited by Sarah Huffman
Music Engraving by Computer Music Services

Includes arrangements by: Don Marsh, Ed Kee, Donny Monk and John DeVries

BRENTWOOD
— MUSIC —

Alphabetical Index of Songs

4

Many of these songs can be found on the following recordings available from Brentwood Music:

TITLE		PRODUCT NO.
America's 25 Favorite Praise & Worship Choruses Vol. 1	Stereo Cass	C-5342
America's 25 Favorite Praise & Worship Choruses Vol. 1	Split-Track Cass	C-5353
America's 25 Favorite Praise & Worship Choruses Vol. 1	Stereo CD	CD-5342
America's 25 Favorite Praise & Worship Choruses Vol. 1	Split-Track	CD-5353
America's 25 Favorite Praise & Worship Choruses Vol. 2	Stereo Cass	C-5401
America's 25 Favorite Praise & Worship Choruses Vol. 2	Split-Track Cass	C- 5470
America's 25 Favorite Praise & Worship Choruses Vol. 2	Stereo CD	CD-5401
America's 25 Favorite Praise & Worship Choruses Vol. 2	Split-Track CD	CD-5470
America's 25 Favorite Praise & Worship Choruses Vol. 3	Stereo Cass	C-5519
America's 25 Favorite Praise & Worship Choruses Vol. 3	Split-Track Cass	C-5520
America's 25 Favorite Praise & Worship Choruses Vol. 3	Stereo CD	CD-5519
America's 25 Favorite Praise & Worship Choruses Vol. 3	Split-Track CD	CD-5520
America's 25 Favorite Praise & Worship Choruses Vol. 4	Stereo Cass	C-5616
America's 25 Favorite Praise & Worship Choruses Vol. 4	Split-Track Cass	C-5629
America's 25 Favorite Praise & Worship Choruses Vol. 4	Stereo CD	CD-5616
America's 25 Favorite Praise & Worship Choruses Vol. 4	Split Track CD	CD-5629
America's 25 Favorite Hymns Vol. 1	Stereo Cass	C-5509
America's 25 Favorite Hymns Vol. 1	Split-Track Cass	C-5516
America's 25 Favorite Hymns Vol. 1	Stereo CD	CD-5509
America's 25 Favorite Hymns Vol. 1	Split-Track CD	CD-5516
America's 25 Favorite Hymns Vol. 2	Stereo Cass	C-5596
America's 25 Favorite Hymns Vol. 2	Split-Track Cass	C-5597
America's 25 Favorite Hymns Vol. 2	Stereo CD	CD-5596
America's 25 Favorite Hymns Vol. 2	Split-Track CD	CD-5597
Created to Praise	Stereo Cass	C-5521
Created to Praise	Stereo CD	CD-5521

How Great Thou Art
(Ps. 48:1)

Words and Music by
STUART K. HINE

Then sings my soul, my Sav-ior God to Thee: How great Thou art, how great Thou art! Then sings my soul, my Sav-ior God to Thee: How great Thou art, how great Thou

Great Is the Lord
(Ps. 48:1)

Words and Music by
MICHAEL W. SMITH and DEBORAH D. SMITH

Bless His Holy Name
(Psalm 103:22)

Words and Music by
ANDRAÉ CROUCH

ho - ly___ name!　　Bless the Lord,___

O my soul,___　and all　that is with - in me, bless His

ho - ly___ name!　name!

We Have Come Into His House

(Ps. 122:1)

Words and Music by
BRUCE BALLINGER

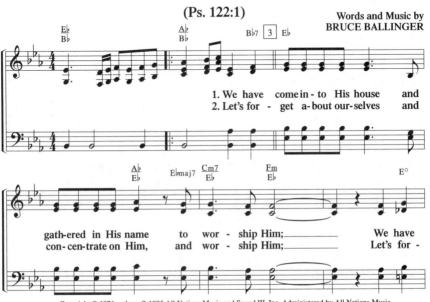

1. We have come in - to His house　　and
2. Let's for - get a - bout our - selves　and

gath-ered in His name　　to wor - ship Him;___　　We have
con - cen-trate on Him,　and wor - ship Him;___　　Let's for -

There's Something About That Name

(Acts 4:12)

Words and Music by
WILLIAM J. and GLORIA GAITHER

Je - sus, Je - sus, Je - sus: there's just some-thing__ a - bout that name—_____ Mas - ter, Sav - ior, Je - sus,_____ like the fra - grance af - ter the rain._____ Je - sus,_____ Je - sus, Je - sus, let all heav - en__ and earth pro -

claim:＿＿＿＿＿＿＿＿＿＿ Kings and king-doms will

all pass a-way, but there's some-thing a-bout that

name.＿＿＿＿＿ name.＿＿＿＿＿

Let's Just Praise the Lord
(Ps. 145:21)

Words and Music by
WILLIAM J. and GLORIA GAITHER

Let's just praise＿＿＿＿ the Lord, praise＿＿＿＿ the

Change My Heart, O God

(Ps. 51:10)

Words and Music by
EDDIE ESPINOSA

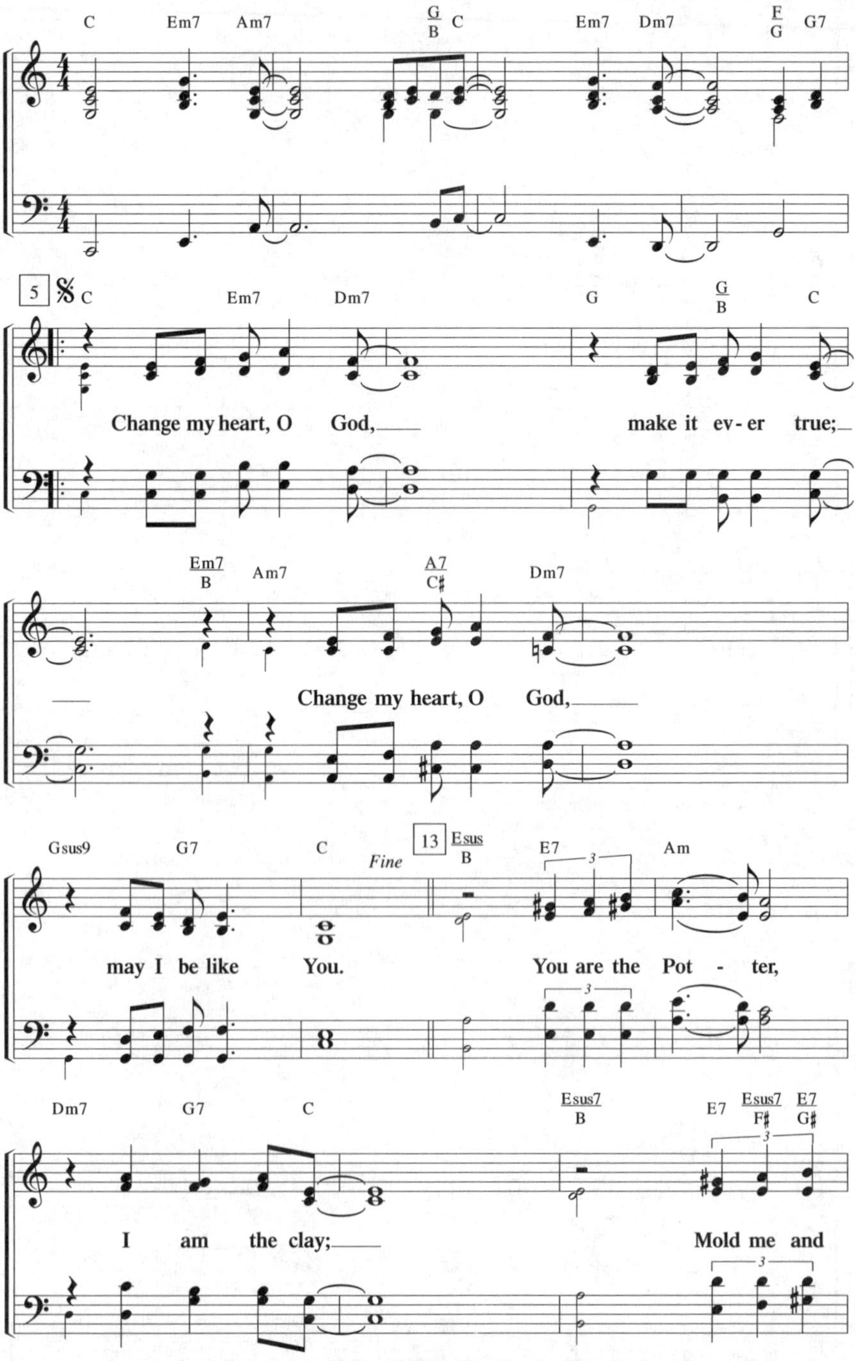
Change my heart, O God,
make it ev-er true;
Change my heart, O God,
may I be like You.
Fine
You are the Pot - ter,
I am the clay;
Mold me and

In Moments Like These
(Ps. 89:1)

Words and Music by
DAVID GRAHAM

16

Surely the Presence of the Lord
(Gen. 28:16)

Words and Music by
LANNY WOLFE

Sure - ly the pres - ence of the Lord is in this place.

Turn Your Eyes Upon Jesus
(2 Cor. 3:18)

Words and Music by
HELEN H. LEMMEL

Turn your eyes up - on Je - sus— Look full in His won - der - ful face;_____ And the things of earth will grow strange - ly dim In the

light of His glo - ry and grace. _____ grace,

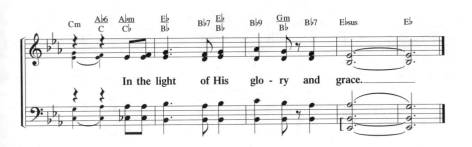

In the light of His glo - ry and grace. _____

Because He Lives
(John 14:19)

Words by
WILLIAM J. and GLORIA GAITHER

Music by
WILLIAM J. GAITHER

Be - cause He __ lives _____

I can face to - mor - row, _____ Be - cause He

Majesty
(Heb. 2:9)

Words and Music by
JACK HAYFORD

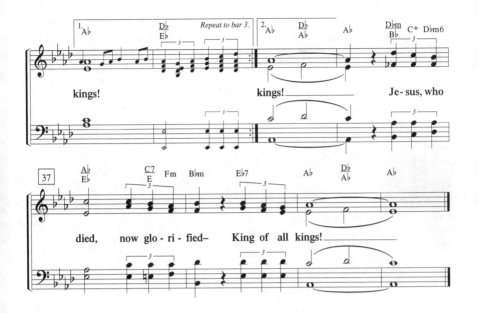

kings! kings! Je- sus, who

died, now glo-ri-fied– King of all kings!

I Will Call Upon the Lord
(Ps. 18:3)

Words and Music by
MICHAEL O'SHIELDS

I will call up-on the Lord
(I will call up-on the

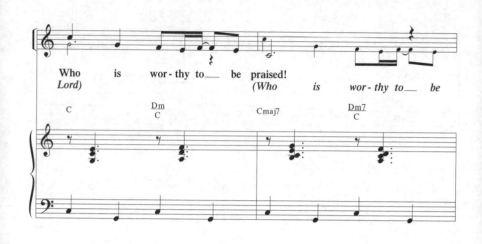

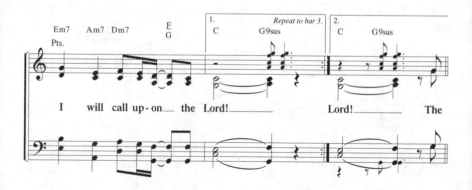

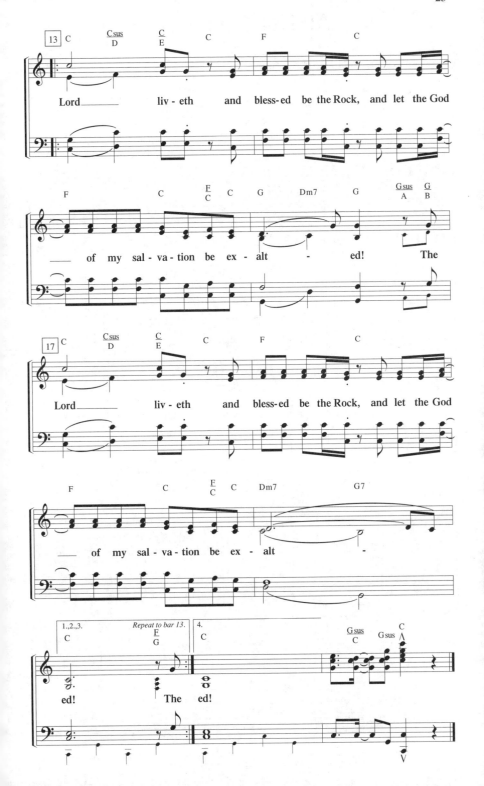

All Hail King Jesus
(Rev. 19:16)

Words and Music by
DAVE MOODY

reign with You through-out e-ter-ni-ty!

Repeat to bar 4.

All hail King__ ty!

Emmanuel
(Isa. 7:14)

Words and Music by
BOB McGEE

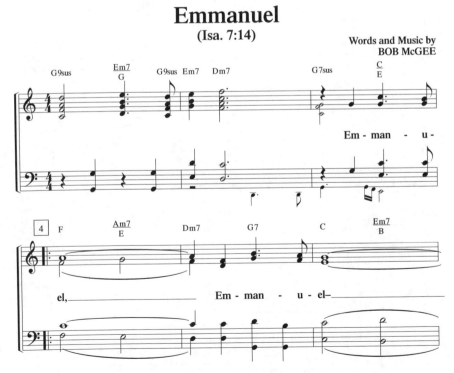

Em - man - u-

el,_____ Em - man - u - el-

28

His Name Is Wonderful
(I Cor. 12:3)

Words and Music by
AUDREY MIEIR

30

How Majestic Is Your Name
(Ps. 8:1)

Words and Music by
MICHAEL W. SMITH

O

Lord,— our Lord,— how ma - jes -tic is Your name— in all— the—

earth!   O earth!   O— Lord,
(Lord, our Lord,—

we praise Your name!   O

Lord, our— Lord,—)

Lord,
(Lord, our Lord,—   Lord, our— Lord,—)

we mag - ni- fy— Your

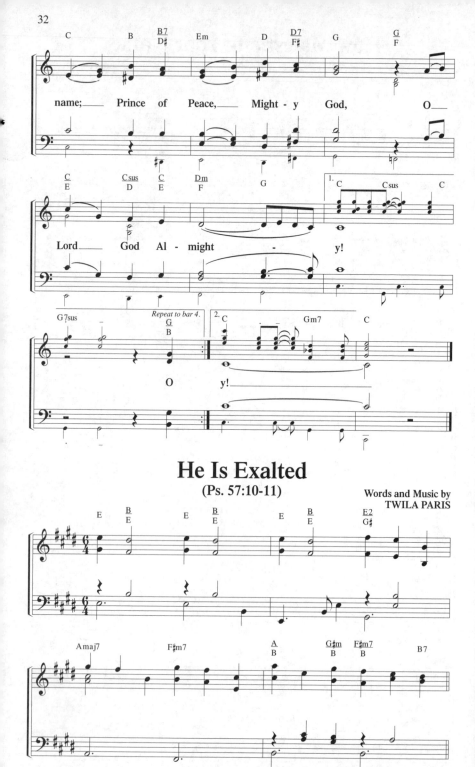

He Is Exalted
(Ps. 57:10-11)

Words and Music by
TWILA PARIS

Lyrics (from staff): name; Prince of Peace, Might-y God, O Lord God Al-might - y! O y!

33

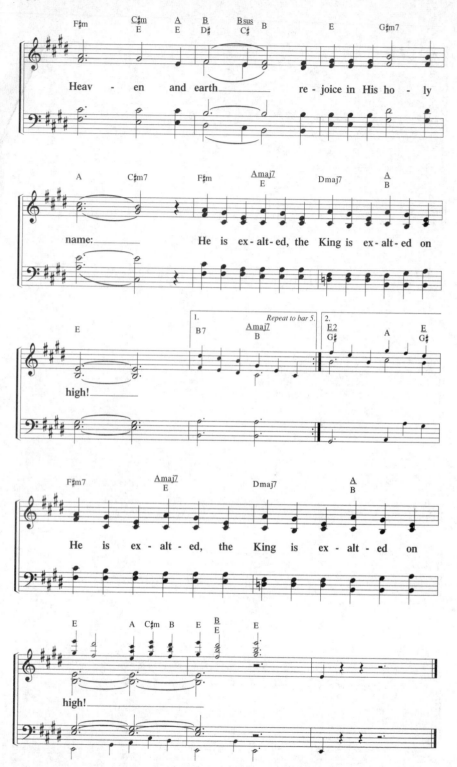

Heav - en and earth__ re - joice in His ho - ly

name:___ He is ex - alt - ed, the King is ex - alt - ed on

high!___

He is ex - alt - ed, the King is ex - alt - ed on

high!___

Praise the Name of Jesus
(Ps. 18:2)

Words and Music by
ROY HICKS, Jr.

We Will Glorify
(Rev. 15:4)

Words and Music by
TWILA PARIS

1. We will glo - ri - fy the King of Kings, we will
(2. Lord Je-) ho - vah reigns in maj - es - ty, we will

glo - ri - fy the Lamb; We will glo - ri - fy the
bow be - fore His throne; We will wor - ship Him in

Lord of Lords, who___ is The Great I Am. 2. Lord Je -
right - eous - ness, we will wor - ship Him a -

Repeat to bar 5.

Ah, Lord God
(Jer. 32:17)

Words and Music by
KAY CHANCE

Awesome God
(Ps. 68:35)

Words and Music by
RICH MULLINS

Our God Reigns
(Isa. 52:7)

Words and Music by
LEONARD E. SMITH

42

Thou Art Worthy
(Rev. 4:11)

Words and Music by
PAULINE MICHAEL MILLS

Thou art wor - thy, Thou art wor - thy,

Thou art wor - thy, O Lord

To re-ceive glo - ry,____ glo - ry and hon - or,

Glo - ry and hon - or and pow'r. For

I Exalt Thee
(Ps. 97:9)

Words and Music by
PETE SANCHEZ, Jr.

Holy Ground
(Ex. 3:5)

Words and Music by
GERON DAVIS

Lyrics:

We are stand - ing _____ on ho - ly ground, _____ And I know that there are an - gels all a - round; _____ Let us _____ praise _____ Je - sus now: _____ We are

stand - ing in His pres - ence on ho - ly ground.

We are ground. We are

stand - ing in His pres - ence on ho - ly ground.

We Bring the Sacrifice of Praise
(Heb. 13:15)

Words and Music by
KIRK DEARMAN

We bring the sac-ri-fice of

praise in-to the house of the Lord;

48

O How He Loves You and Me
(John 15:9)

Words and Music by
KURT KAISER

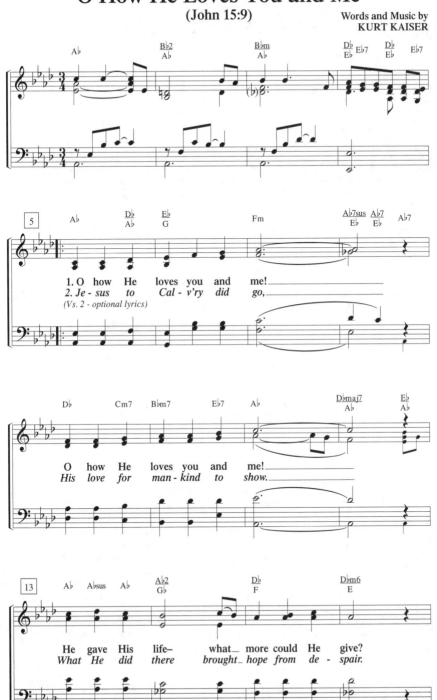

1. O how He loves you and me!
2. Je - sus to Cal - v'ry did go,

(Vs. 2 - optional lyrics)

O how He loves you and me!
His love for man - kind to show.

He gave His life— what more could He give?
What He did there brought hope from de - spair.

O how He loves you— O how He loves me—

O how He loves you and me!

Repeat to bar 5.

O how He loves you and me!

Lord, Be Glorified
(2 Thess. 1:12)

Words and Music by
BOB KILPATRICK

1. In my life, Lord,— be glo-ri-fied,

be glo-ri-fied;— In my life, Lord,— be glo-ri-fied to-

day._____ 2. In my home, Lord,___ be glo-ri-fied,

be glo-ri-fied;___ In my home, Lord,___ be glo-ri-fied___ to-

day.___ 3. In Your church, Lord,___

be glo-ri-fied, be glo-ri-fied;___ In Your church, Lord,___

be glo-ri-fied___ to-day, be glo-ri-fied___ to-day.

Come, Give Glory to the Lord
(Psalm 93:1; 96:8-10)

Words and Music by
ED KEE

For Me, To Live Is Christ
(Phil. 1:21)

Words by
GARY MATHENA and ED KEE

Music by
GARY MATHENA

In Your Presence
(Rev. 7:9-12)

Words and Music by
NANCY GORDON

In Your pres - ence, Lord,_____ there is splen - dor._____ In Your pres - ence, Lord,_____ we sur - ren - der. In Your pres - ence, Lord,_____ we bow be - fore_____ You_____ to a - dore_____ You,_____ to be - hold_____ You_____ as Lord and King._____

Love Beyond Degree
(Rom. 5:10, 11)

Words and Music by
ED KEE and BRIAN CARR

Love be - yond de - gree,_____ suf - fer-
sin there was a cost:_____ Your death up -

ing for me;_____ In the bread You
on the cross._____ Out of love, You

1.
gave to me, I see Your pain. For my
suf - fered

2.
loss that I should_____ gain.

Repeat to bar 5.

Not to Us
(Psalm 115:1)

Words and Music by
NANCY GORDON

Song of Thanksgiving
(Ps. 101:1)

Words and Music by
ED KEE

In the Spirit of Worship
(Ps. 5:7)

Words and Music by
NANCY GORDON

Mighty King
(Ps.98:1-3)

Words and Music by
NANCY GORDON

Through the Blood

(Col. 1:12-14)

Words and Music by
ED KEE and DALE MATHEWS

1. Blood of Je - sus, shed for me;
2. If all sin were mine a - lone,
3. By the Fa - ther's plan di - vine,
4. I shall see Him face to face,

Pre - cious blood, my cov - 'ring be. The
Je - sus' blood would still a - tone.
there's a prom - ise He's de - signed:
prais - ing God; For by His grace,

4th time to CODA
(to bar 19)

on - ly view God has of me is
I've been made God's ver - y own
That His life is one with mine,
all my sin has been e - rased

through the blood of Je -

rit. last time

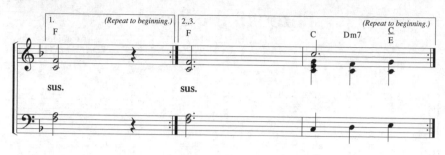

sus.   sus.

♦ CODA

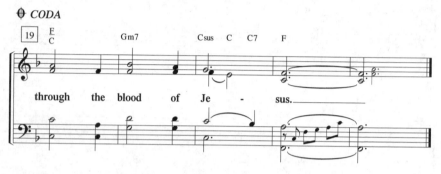

through   the   blood   of   Je - sus.____

This Is the House of the Lord
(Ps. 135:1-3)

Words and Music by
RUSSELL MAULDIN

This   is the house   of   the   Lord,____

en - ter   with hearts   in   ac - cord;_____   And ac-

know-ledge the pres-ence of the One we a - dore, for this is the house of the Lord.

Thou Art Worthy
(Rev. 4:11)

Words and Music by
RUSSELL MAULDIN

Thou art wor-thy, Thou art wor-thy, Thou art wor-thy, Thou art wor-thy. Thou art wor-thy of glo - ry and hon - or and pow'r, for Thou hast cre-at - ed all things.

We'll Call Him Jesus
(Isa. 9:6)

Words and Music by
KAREN DEAN

We'll call Him Je - sus, the name the an - gels whis - pered.

We'll call Him Je - sus, come from heav'n to be our friend.

We'll call Him Je - sus, the sweet - est name in all the world.

We'll call Him Je - sus, He'll save us from our sin.

But when your heart is full of joy, you'll call Him "Won - der - ful."

Break Me, Lord
(Phil. 2:5; Col. 3:1-4)

Words and Music by
STEVE JONES

1. Break me, Lord,_____ take my will a-way;_____ Help me
(2.) Lord,_____ take my pride from me;_____ Help me

learn to say,_____ "Thy will be done."_____ Let Your
yield to Thee,_____ and self ig-nore._____ When my

plans for me_____ and my own de-sires be one._____
heart is cold_ and made of stone, please break me, Lord._____

Take my life, make it Yours a-lone;_____ Ev-'ry-

thing I own_____ be-longs to You._____ Let me glo-ri-fy_ Je-sus

Do You Love Me?
(John 21:15-17)

Words and Music by
STEVE JONES

Heart of a Servant
(Mark 9:35)

Words and Music by
ED KEE and BRIAN CARR

1. Give me a heart of com-pas-sion,____ give me a heart to care.
2. Give me a heart____ of mer-cy____ to do____ the things You do.

Je-sus, through You,____ make all that I do____ be just as if You____ were there.

Give me the heart of a ser-vant,

(Repeat to beginning.)

Lord;____ Place in me the heart of You;____

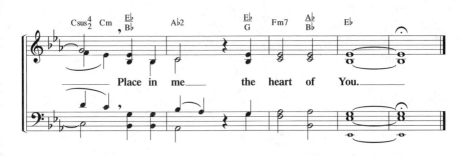

Sing Aloud
(Ps. 81:1)

Words and Music by
NANCY GORDON

70

Descant

Sing a - loud loud with a joy - ful voice. Sing a -

sing a - loud loud, let your praise be heard. Sing a -

Sing a - loud and de - loud, pro - claim His love and de -

1. Repeat to bar 1. 2.
clare His ho - ly Word. Word.

1. Repeat to bar 1. 2.
Em Em
clare His ho - ly Word. 2. He will Word.

Praise to You
(Ps. 146:2)

Words and Music by
ED KEE and BRIAN CARR

Lord, let me lift my praise to You;

No oth- er gift– just praise to You.____

Lord, while I live, all I can give____ is

praise to____ You. If the

trees of the field____ re- joice,____ and

72

O Lord, Our God
(Ps. 93:1; 104:1-5)

Words and Music by
M. SPARROW HOLT

We Will Praise the Name of the Lord

(Ps. 148:13)

Words and Music by
ED KEE

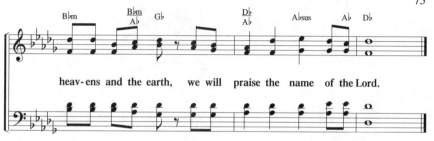

heav-ens and the earth, we will praise the name of the Lord.

Thy Loving Kindness
(Ps. 63:3)

Words and Music by
HUGH MITCHELL

Optional counter-melody *(2nd time only)*

Thy lov-ing - kind - ness

Thy lov-ing - kind - ness___ is bet-ter than

is bet-ter than life, Thy lov-ing -

life,___ Thy lov-ing - kind - ness

This Is the Day
(Ps. 118:24)

Words and Music by
LES GARRETT

this is the day that the Lord has made!

made, That the Lord has made!

As You Go About
(Matt.28:19-20)

Words by
BILL O'BRIEN, ROB SELLERS and BILL CATES

Music by
BILL CATES

As you go a-bout, as you go,

Take the name of Him who loves you so.

By His pow- er and com- mand, go dis- ci - ple ev-'ry man;___

As you go a-bout,___ as you go.

Drawn Together by His Love
(Eph. 4:3-5)

Words and Music by
BILL CATES

Drawn to-geth-er by His love,___ drawn to-geth-er by the

Spir- it of the Lord;___ Drawn to-geth- er by His

love,___ we are one in the Spir- it___ of God.

How Blessed
(Ps. 1:1-3)

Words and Music by
CLAY CLARKSON

How blessed is the man whose de-light is in the law of the Lord.

He med-i-tates day___ and night,___ feed-ing up-on___ God's Word.

Repeat to bar 1. *Fine*

1. He does not walk where the wick-
2. He will be like a grow-

ed walk, or stand___ where the sin-ners stand;___
ing tree- plant-ed by a flow-ing stream;___

He does not sit where the mock - ers talk, but
Pros-per-ing___ in all___ he does

Blessed Is the Lord
(Ps. 106:48)

Words and Music by
ED KEE

1. Bless - ed is the Lord, our
2. Bless - ed is the Lord, our
3. Bless - ed is the Lord, our

1. God— awe - some and great, for - ev - er the same.
2. strength— in heav - en and earth Your pow - er we claim.
3. hope— Re - deem - er of men, You've tak - en our shame.

Bless - ed is the Lord, our might - y rock; We praise and ex - alt Your
Bless - ed is the Lord, Who o - ver - comes; We praise and ex - alt Your
Bless - ed is the Lord, our right - eous - ness; We praise and ex - alt Your

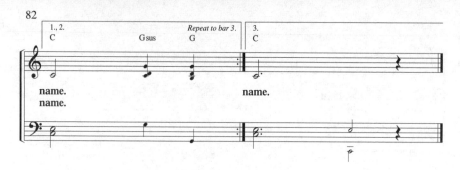

My Highest Aim
(I Thess. 2:4b)

Words and Music by
NANCY GORDON

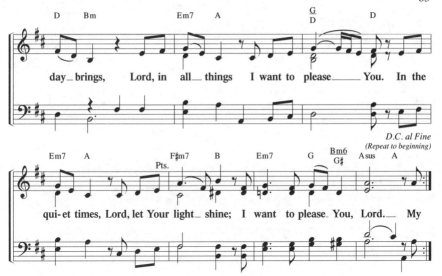

When I Wait Upon the Lord

(Isa. 40:31)

Words and Music by
BARBIE LOFLIN

When I wait up-on the
I will wait up-on the

1. Repeat to beginning

2.

Lord.
Lord.

We Need Jesus
(John 15:4-5)

Words and Music by
WAYNE and ELIZABETH GOODINE

We need Je-sus, how we need Je-sus—

He's our hope and rea-son to be-lieve. We need Je-sus, our world needs

Je-sus— He's the an-swer to our ev-'ry need.

O God, You Are Mighty

(Zeph. 3:17)

Words and Music by
NANCY GORDON

I Commit Myself to Thee
(Ps. 37:5)

Words and Music by
PAMELA SHIRLEY

I com-mit my-self to Thee, O Lord: All that I have I give to Thee, O Lord. Take my life, my will, my ev-'ry-thing, O Lord. Un-fail-ing love sur-rounds me when I place my trust in ho-ly hands. All that I am, all that I will

be,   I com - mit it, Lord, to Thee.

Speak His Name
(Matt. 1:23)

Words by
KAREN DEAN and DON MARSH

Music by
DON MARSH

Speak His name,   speak His name; Speak the love - ly name of Je - sus.   God is with us,   call Him Em - man - u - el,   Em - man - u - el.   man - u - el.

Repeat to bar 5.

Glorious Is Your Name
(Ps. 72:19)

Words and Music by
NANCY GORDON and DENNIS ALLEN

Your Highest Joy
(Eph. 5:18)

Words and Music by
RANDY ALAN

Savior, Healer, Friend
(John 15:15b)

Words and Music by
KAREN DEAN and DON MARSH

1. Sav - ior, Heal - er, Friend, _____ mer - cy
2. Ev - 'ry sin and stain, _____ sick - ness,

with - out end– I find all I
grief and pain, And my lone - li -

need, ev - 'ry - thing in my Sav - ior,
ness

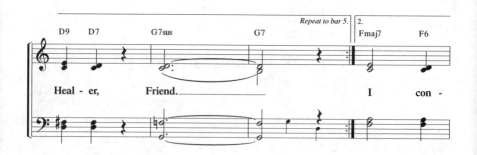

Heal - er, Friend. I con -

Repeat to bar 5.

fess to my Sav - ior, Heal - er, Friend.

Lead Me, Lord
(John 10:27)

Words and Music by
WAYNE and ELIZABETH GOODINE

I Find My Peace in You
(Isa. 26:3)

Words and Music by
WAYNE and ELIZABETH GOODINE

I find my peace in You, Lord,

I find my strength in Your name;

I find my peace in You, Lord,

when this old world brings me pain.

When my heart's filled with sor - row,

Seems I can't find my way,

I find my peace in You, Lord,

I find my strength in Your name.

Though Your Sins Be As Scarlet
(Isa. 1:18)

Words and Music by
WAYNE GOODINE

Though your sins be as scar - let, they shall

be __ as __ wool; Though they be red __ as

crim - son, they shall be white as snow.

Come Sing
(Ps. 95:1-2)

Words and Music by
NANCY GORDON

Come sing, __ come bless the Lord, __ let your joys __ be

known. __ Come sing, __ come bless the Lord, __ let

Suggested intro

3rd time to CODA ✛
(to bar 18)

praise __ sur - round His throne. __

1. We ap - plaud __ Your
2. You de - feat __ our

tri-umphs,___ we mar-vel at___ Your might.
en-e-mies___ and e-vil has___ to flee.

We an-nounce___ Your truth, O Lord, and dark-ness turns___ to
You've be-come___ our con-fi-dence, our hope, our vic-to-

Light!
ry.

praise___ sur-round___ His throne.___

Let praise___ sur-round___ His throne.

My Soul Doth Magnify the Lord
(Luke 1:46-47)

Words and Music by
DAVE CLARK

My soul doth mag-ni-fy the Lord. My

soul doth mag - ni - fy the Lord.____ My spir - it re - joic - es in

God my Sav - ior, for my soul doth mag - ni - fy the Lord.

I'm Free
(Gal. 5:1)

Words and Music by
WAYNE GOODINE

I'm free,____ I'm free! Je - sus'

blood now cov - ers me.__ From the load of sin that

so long I car - ried, I'm free, I'm free! Thank God, I'm free.

I Sent You to Reap

(John 4:35-38)

Words and Music by
STEVE JONES

He Really Cares for You
(Matt. 11:29)

Words and Music by
WAYNE GOODINE

Lift High His Banner
(Ps. 20:5)

Words and Music by
NANCY GORDON

1. Lift high His ban - ner, let the trum - pet sound.
2. Lift high His ban - ner, shout the vic - to - ry.

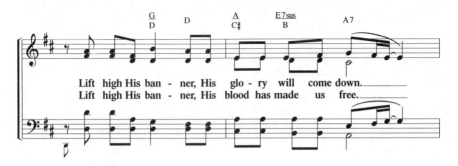

Lift high His ban - ner, His glo - ry will come down.
Lift high His ban - ner, His blood has made us free.

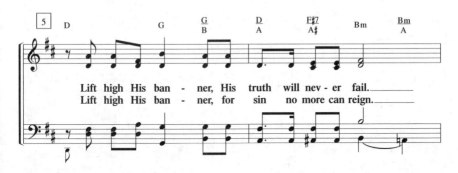

Lift high His ban - ner, His truth will nev - er fail.
Lift high His ban - ner, for sin no more can reign.

Suggested intro

Repeat to beginning.

Lift high His ban - ner, let right-eous - ness pre-vail.
Lift high His ban - ner, come

Send Us Out
(Acts 4:31)

Words and Music by
MARTY PARKS

We have met in Your pres-ence, we have wor-shipped in Your name; We have
felt Your Ho-ly Spir-it in this hour. And we
part de-clar-ing all the might-y things that You have done; Send us
out in Your love and in Your pow'r,____ Send us
out in Your love and in Your pow'r.____

In One Accord
(Phil. 2:1-2)

Words and Music by
JACK BRADY, Jr.

Sanctuary
(Eph. 2:19-22)

Words and Music by
JOHN W. THOMPSON
and RANDY L. SCRUGGS

Yes, Lord, Yes
(I Sam. 15:22)

Words and Music by
LYNN KEESECKER

Purified Heart
(Ps. 27:4)

Words and Music by
MARK HAUTH and DAVID McMULLAN

1. Lord, I long to see You— all the beau-ty You hold;
2. When I see my own life, sin can dark-en the view;

If I could look deep in Your heart I'd find treas-ures un -
Yet, Your prom-ise still lights my way and stands for-ev-er

told, worth more than all the world's gold.
true— Your grace will car-ry me through.

You are ho-ly, pure in heart— Je-sus, show me all that You are.

Change me com-plete-ly, cleanse ev-'ry part, 'til Your love flows from a

sugg. intro

Give Me a Faithful Heart
(Rom. 1:16)

Words and Music by
**VINCE WILCOX, JEFF NELSON
and LYNN WHITE**

There Is a Redeemer
(Eph. 1:7)

Words and Music by
MELODY GREEN

leav - ing Your Spir - it 'til the work on earth is done.

I Praise You, Lord
(Rev. 1:16)

Words and Music by
BARBIE LOFLIN and ED KEE

Fair - est of mil - lions, love - li - est of all; Hum - bled in Your pres - ence, on my knees I fall To wor - ship and a - dore You, ho - ly, gra - cious King.

Flow Out
(Rev. 22:1-2)

Words and Music by
NANCY GORDON

Wait Upon the Lord
(Isa. 40:31)

Words and Music by
DAN WILLIAMS

114

Merciful, Almighty God
(Jer. 17:12)

Words and Music by
MARION MEDINA and TED B. WILSON

By Him, For Him
(Col. 1:16)

Words and Music by
RICK BLAIR

He is wor-thy of wor-ship and praise. It was
by_____ Him, for_____ Him— Je-sus cre-at-ed all
things for His wor-ship and praise._____

Wonderful Is Your Name
(Isa. 9:6)

Words and Music by
MARION MEDINA

O ho-ly Lord,_____ Glo-rious
One that we sing_____ to, Je-sus we praise_____ You. O ho-ly Lord.

118

You Are Worthy

(Rev. 4:11)

Words and Music by
ELIZABETH GOODINE

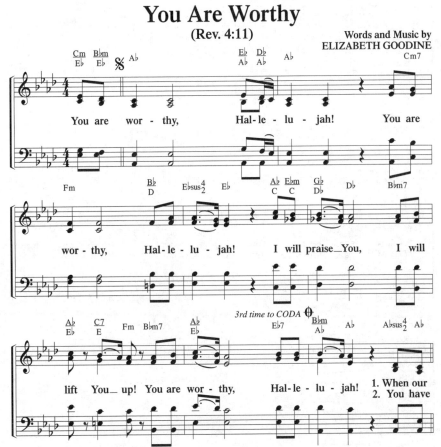

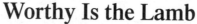

Worthy Is the Lamb
(Rev. 5:12)

Words and Music by
JEFF NELSON

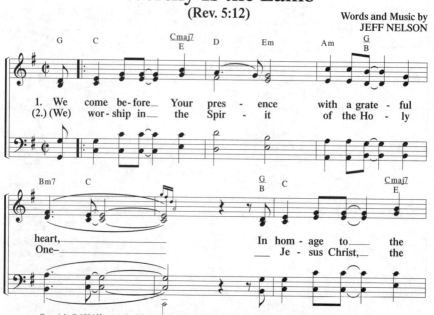

122

Holy Spirit, Thou Art Welcome

(I Cor. 6:17)

Words and Music by
DAVID HUNTSINGER and DOTTIE RAMBO

Where the Spirit of the Lord Is
(II Cor. 3:17)

Words and Music by
STEVE ADAMS

Just As I Am

(John 6:37)

CHARLOTTE ELLIOTT   WILLIAM B. BRADBURY

1. Just____ as I am,____ with-out____ one plea But
2. Just____ as I am,____ and wait - ing not To
3. Just____ as I am,____ Thou wilt____ re - ceive, Wilt

that____ Thy blood was shed for me, And____
rid____ my soul of one dark blot, To____
wel - come, par - don, cleanse, re - lieve; Be -

that Thou bidd'st____ me come____ to____ Thee,
Thee Whose blood____ can cleanse____ each____ spot,____ O Lamb of
cause Thy prom - ise I be - lieve,____

God,____ I come! I____ come!

Oh, the Glory of Your Presence
(II Chron. 5:14)

Words and Music by
STEVE FRY

Lift Up Your Heads
(Ps. 24:7-8)

Words and Music by
STEVE FRY

Sweet, Sweet Spirit
(Gal. 5:22)

Words and Music by
DORIS MAE AKERS

There's a sweet, sweet Spir - it in this place,_____ And I know that it's the Spir - it of___ the Lord;_____ There are
(There are) sweet sweet ex - press - ions on each face,_____ And I know that it's the pres - ence of___ the Lord._____ Sweet Ho - ly Spir - it, Sweet heav-en-ly Dove, Stay right here with___ us,

Fill-ing us with Your love;____ And for these bless-ings We

lift our hearts in praise:____ With-out a doubt we'll know that we have

been re-vived,__ When we shall leave this place.____

Fairest Lord Jesus
(Isa. 33:17)

from Münster Gesangbuch

CRUSADER'S HYMN
Silesian Folk Melody

1. Fair - est Lord Je - sus, Rul - er of all na - ture,
2. Fair are the mead - ows, Fair - er still the wood - lands,
3. Beau - ti - ful Sav - ior! Lord____ of the na - tions!

O____ Thou of__ God____ and__ man the Son:
Robed__ in__ the_ bloom - ing garb of spring:
Son__ of____ God____ and__ Son of Man!

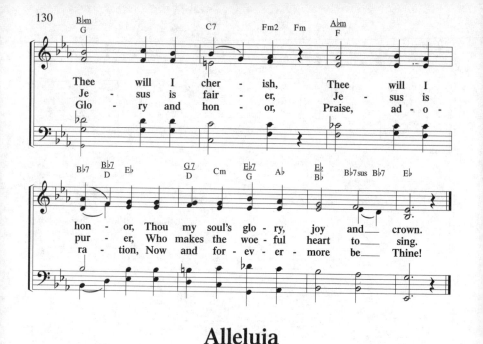

Thee will I cher- ish, Thee will I
Je- sus is fair- er, Je- sus is
Glo- ry and hon- or, Praise, ad- o-

hon- or, Thou my soul's glo- ry, joy and crown.
pur- er, Who makes the woe- ful heart to sing.
ra- tion, Now and for- ev- er- more be Thine!

Alleluia
(Rev. 19:1)

Words and Music by
JERRY SINCLAIR

1. Al- le- lu ia, Al- le- lu- ia, Al- le- lu ia, Al- le-
(2. He is) wor- thy, Al- le- lu- ia, He is wor- thy, Al- le-
(3. I will) praise Him, Al- le- lu- ia, I will praise Him, Al- le-

lu- ia. Al- le- lu ia, Al- le- lu ia, Al- le-
lu- ia. He is wor- thy, Al- le- lu- ia, He is
lu- ia. I will praise Him, Al- le- lu- ia, I will

lu ia, Al- le- lu ia. 2. He is
wor- thy, Al- le- lu- ia. 3. I will
praise Him, Al- le- lu- ia.

Spirit of the Living God
(Gal. 5:16)

Words and Music by
DANIEL IVERSON

Spir - it of the Liv - ing God, fall___ fresh on me.

Spir - it of the Liv - ing God, fall___ fresh on me.

Melt___ me,___ mold me, fill___ me, use___ me.___

Spir - it of the Liv - ing God, fall___ fresh on me.

The Greatest Thing
(Phil. 4:8-10)

Words and Music by
MARK PENDERGRASS

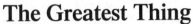
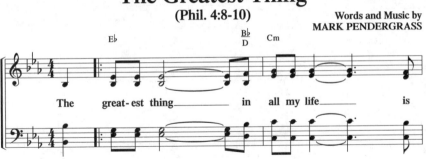

The great - est thing___ in all my life___ is

132

Great and Mighty
(Jer. 32:18-19)

Words and Music by
MARLENE BIGLEY

Great and might - y is the Lord our God, great and might - y is

He; Great and might - y is the Lord our God,

great and might - y is He! Lift your ban - ner, let the

an-thems ring prais - es to our King; Great and might - y is the

Lord our God, great and might - y is He.

I'm Thankful
(Ps. 118:28)

Words and Music by
WAYNE GOODINE

Great Is Thy Faithfulness

(Lam. 3:22-23)

THOMAS O. CHISHOLM   WILLIAM M. RUNYAN

1. Great is Thy faith - ful - ness, O God my Fa - ther,
2. Par - don for sin and a peace that en - dur - eth,

There is no shad - ow of turn - ing with Thee;
Thine own dear pres - ence to cheer and to guide;

Thou chang - est not, Thy com - pas - sions they fail not;
Strength for to - day and bright hope for to - mor - row,

As Thou hast been Thou for - ev - er wilt be.
Bless - ings all mine, with ten thou - sand be - side!

Great is Thy faith - ful - ness! Great is Thy faith - ful - ness!

Morn - ing by morn - ing new mer - cies I see;

All I have need - ed Thy hand hath pro - vid - ed—

Great is Thy faith - ful - ness, Lord, un - to me!

Put Your Life Into the Master's Hand
(Matt. 11:28)

Words and Music by
WAYNE and ELIZABETH GOODINE

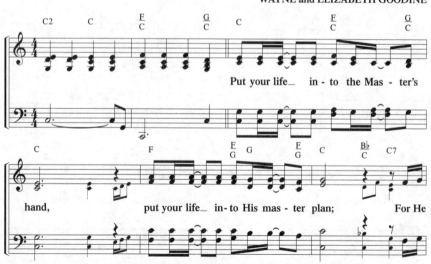

Put your life— in - to the Mas - ter's

hand, put your life— in - to His mas - ter plan; For He

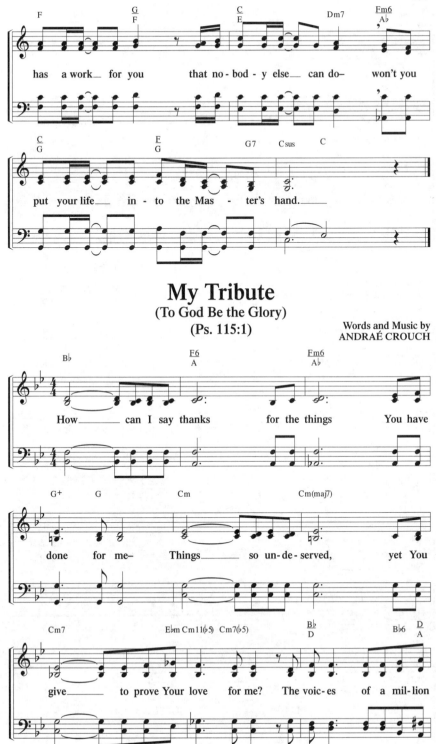

has a work for you that no-bod-y else can do— won't you
put your life in-to the Mas-ter's hand.

My Tribute
(To God Be the Glory)
(Ps. 115:1)

Words and Music by
ANDRAÉ CROUCH

How can I say thanks for the things You have
done for me— Things so un-de-served, yet You
give to prove Your love for me? The voic-es of a mil-lion

138

* On introduction, hold 4 beats.

Emmanuel
(Matt. 1:23)

Words and Music by
JEFF NELSON

1. Won - der - ful Sav - ior, Son of for - ev - er, from
(2.) (Bless - ed Re) - deem - er, Cov - e - nant Keep - er, Your

age to age__ You are__ the same! Glo - ri - ous Je - sus, sent to re-
song of love__ will ev - er reign!__ Pre - cious Je - sus, faith - ful to

deem us, we de - light to speak Your ho - ly name:__ Em-
heal us, for - ev - er we__ will sing Your praise:__ Em-

man - u - el,__ Em - man - u - el.__ Em-
(Em - man - u - el,)

Glo-ri-ous Je-sus, sent to re-deem us, we de-
Pre-cious Je-sus, faith-ful to heal us, for-ev-

light to speak Your ho-ly name. 2. Bless-ed Re-
er we will sing Your

praise. For-ev-er we will sing Your praise.

Praise You
(Ps. 52:9)

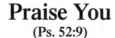

Words and Music by
ELIZABETH GOODINE

Praise You, (praise You,) praise You, Let my

The Steadfast Love of the Lord

(Lam. 3:22-23)

Words and Music by
EDITH McNEILL

new ev-'ry morn-ing, new ev-'ry morn-ing; Great is Thy faith-ful-

ness, O Lord,____ Great is Thy faith-ful - ness.

O For a Thousand Tongues
(Ps. 35:28)

CHARLES WESLEY

CARL G. GLÄZER

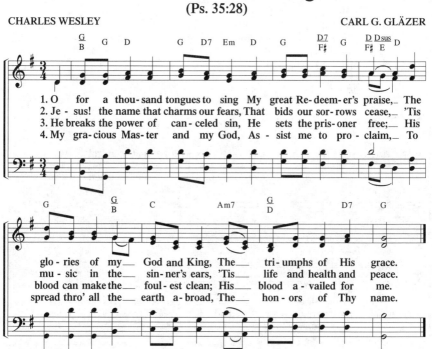

1. O for a thou-sand tongues to sing My great Re-deem-er's praise,_ The
2. Je - sus! the name that charms our fears, That bids our sor-rows cease,_ 'Tis
3. He breaks the power of can-celed sin, He sets the pris-oner free;_ His
4. My gra-cious Mas-ter and my God, As-sist me to pro-claim,_ To

glo-ries of my__ God and King, The__ tri-umphs of His grace.
mu-sic in the__ sin-ner's ears, 'Tis__ life and health and peace.
blood can make the__ foul-est clean; His__ blood a-vailed for me.
spread thro' all the__ earth a-broad, The__ hon-ors of Thy name.

Holy, Holy, Holy
(Rev. 4:8)

REGINALD HEBER   JOHN B. DYKES

Joyful, Joyful, We Adore Thee
(Ps. 139:14)

HENRY VAN DYKE

LUDWIG VAN BEETHOVEN

1. Joy - ful, joy - ful, we a - dore Thee, God of glo - ry,
2. All Thy works with joy sur - round Thee, Earth and heaven re -
3. Mor - tals, join the hap - py cho - rus Which the morn - ing

Lord of love; Hearts un - fold like flowers be - fore Thee,
flect Thy rays, Stars and an - gels sing a - round Thee,
stars be - gan; Fa - ther love is reign - ing o'er us,

Open - ing to the sun a - bove. Melt the clouds of
Cen - ter of un - brok - en praise. Field and for - est,
Broth - er love binds man to man. Ev - er sing - ing,

sin and sad - ness, Drive the dark of doubt a - way;
vale and moun - tain, Flow - ery mead - ow, flash - ing sea,
march we on - ward, Vic - tors in the midst of strife,

Giv - er of im - mor - tal glad - ness, Fill us with the light of day.
Chant - ing bird and flow - ing foun - tain, Call us to re - joice in Thee.
Joy - ful mu - sic leads us sun - ward In the tri - umph song of life.

Praise to the Lord, the Almighty

JOACHIM NEANDER (Dan. 4:37) *Stralsund Gesangbuch*, 1665

1. Praise to the Lord, the Al-might-y, the King of cre-a-tion! O my soul, praise Him, for He is thy health and sal-va-tion! All ye who hear, now to His tem-ple draw near; Join me in glad ad-o-ra-tion.

2. Praise to the Lord! O let all that is in me a-dore Him! All that hath life and breath, come now with prais-es be-fore Him. Let the A-men Sound from His peo-ple a-gain: Glad-ly for aye we a-dore Him.

All Hail the Power of Jesus' Name

(Phil. 2:9-11)

EDWARD PERRONET;
adapted by John Rippon

OLIVER HOLDEN

1. All hail the pow'r of Je - sus' name! Let an - gels pros-trate fall; Bring forth the roy - al di - a - dem, And crown Him Lord of all; Bring forth the roy - al di - a - dem, And crown Him Lord of all!
2. Let ev - 'ry kin - dred, ev - 'ry tribe on this ter - res - trial ball, To Him all maj - es - ty as - cribe, And crown Him Lord of all; To Him all maj - es - ty as - cribe, And crown Him Lord of all!
3. O that with yon - der sa - cred throng We at His feet may fall! We'll join the ev - er - last - ing song, And crown Him Lord of all; We'll join the ev - er - last - ing song, And crown Him Lord of all!

Blessed Assurance

(James 5:13)

FANNY J. CROSBY

PHOEBE P. KNAPP

1. Bless-ed as-sur-ance, Je-sus is mine! O what a fore-taste of glo-ry di-vine! Heir of sal-va-tion, pur-chase of God, Born of His Spir-it, washed in His blood.

2. Per-fect sub-mis-sion– all is at rest, I in my Sav-ior am hap-py and blest; Watch-ing and wait-ing, look-ing a-bove, Filled with His good-ness, lost in His love.

This is my sto-ry, this is my song, *(This is my song)* Prais-ing my

Sav - ior all the day long;____ This is my sto - ry, this is my
song,____ Prais - ing my Sav - ior all the day long.____
(This is my song)

Oh, What a Beautiful Name
(Phil 2:9)

Words and Music by
JANET McMAHAN-WILSON

1. Oh, what a beau - ti - ful name!____ Oh, what a beau - ti - ful
2. Oh, what a won - der - ful Lord!____ Oh, what a won - der - ful

name!____ Je - sus, Je - sus,
Lord!____ Je - sus, Je - sus,

Oh, what a beau - ti - ful____ name!
Oh, what a won - der - ful____

Lord!

My Savior's Love

(I Stand Amazed in the Presence)
(Mark 2:12)

Words and Music by
CHARLES H. GABRIEL

1. I stand a-mazed in the pres - ence Of Je - sus, the Naz - a -
2. He took my sins and my sor - rows, He made them His ver - y

rene,   And won-der how He could love me, A sin - ner, con-demned, un -
own;   He bore the bur - den to Cal - v'ry, And suf - fered and died a -

clean.
lone.   How mar - vel - ous! how won - der - ful!

And my song shall ev - er be: How mar - vel - ous!

how won - der - ful Is my Sav - ior's love for me!

The Old Rugged Cross
(Phil. 2:8)

Words and Music by
GEORGE BENNARD

1. On a hill far a-way stood an old rug-ged cross, The em-blem of suf-'ring and shame; And I love that old cross where the dear-est and best For a world of lost sin-ners was slain. So I'll cher-ish the old rug-ged cross, Till my

2. To the old rug-ged cross I will ev-er be true, Its shame and re-proach glad-ly bear; Then He'll call me some day to my home far a-way, Where His glo-ry for-ev-er I'll share.

152

tro - phies at last I lay down;____ I will

cling to the old rug - ged cross,_____ And ex-

change it some-day for a crown._____

A Call to Praise
(Ps. 92:1)

Words and Music by
JOHN LEMONIS and DONNA CITY

I bow___ my heart, I bend___ my knees,_____ I

wor-ship You___ in all Your maj - es - ty. I lift___ my voice, I raise___ my

hands,_____ I'm here to give___ You ev - 'ry - thing___ I

am._____ You___ are ho - ly, You___ are might - y,_____

You are wor - thy of__ my praise.____ You are right - eous, You reign___ in

glo - ry; You are wel - come in___ this place.

O Lord, You're Beautiful
(I Chron. 16:2)

Words and Music by
KEITH GREEN

O Lord, You're beau - ti - ful; Your

face is all I seek. And when___ Your

eyes___ are on this child, Your grace a -

bounds___ to me.___ O me.___

I Will Magnify
(Ps. 34:3)

Words and Music by
MICHAEL PASSONS, JEFF NELSON
and JEFFREY DEAN

I will mag - ni - fy___ Je - sus Christ,_ my King;_

'Tis So Sweet to Trust in Jesus
(John 14:1)

LOUISA M. R. STEAD

WILLIAM J. KIRKPATRICK

1. 'Tis so sweet to trust in Je - sus, Just to take Him at His word,___ Just to rest up - on His prom - ise, Just to know "Thus saith the Lord."
2. I'm so glad I learned to trust Him, Pre - cious Je - sus, Sav - ior, Friend;___ And I know that He is with me, Will be with me to the end.

Je - sus, Je - sus, how I trust Him! How I've proved Him o'er and o'er! Je - sus, Je - sus, pre - cious Je - sus! O for grace___ to trust Him more!

I Need Thee Every Hour

ANNIE S. HAWKS;
ROBERT LOWRY, refrain

(Ps. 86:1)

ROBERT LOWRY

Holy Ground

(Heb. 12:22-24)

Words and Music by
CHRISTOPHER BEATTY

What a Friend We Have in Jesus
(Phil. 4:6)

JOSEPH M. SCRIVEN

CHARLES C. CONVERSE

1. What a Friend we have in Je - sus, All our sins and griefs to bear! What a priv - i - lege to car - ry Ev - 'ry-thing to God in prayer! O what peace we of - ten for - feit, O what need-less pain we bear, All be - cause we do not car - ry Ev - 'ry-thing to God in prayer.

2. Have we tri - als and temp - ta - tions? Is there trou - ble an - y-where? We should nev - er be dis - cour - aged, Take it to the Lord in prayer. Can we find a friend so faith - ful Who will all our sor - rows share? Je - sus knows our ev - 'ry weak - ness, Take it to the Lord in prayer.

In the Garden
(John 20:20)

Words and Music by
C. AUSTIN MILES

1. I come to the gar-den a-lone,__ While the dew is still on the ros-es; And the voice I hear, fall-ing on my ear, The Son of God dis-clos-es.

2. He speaks, and the sound of His voice__ Is so sweet the birds hush their sing-ing; And the mel-o-dy that He gave to me With-in my heart is ring-ing.

And He walks with me and He talks with me, And He tells me I am His own;____ And the joy__ we share as we tar-ry there None oth-er has ev-er__ known.__

With My Whole Heart
(Ps. 119:10)

Words and Music by
BILLY CROCKETT and KENNY WOOD

I Know That My Redeemer Lives
(Job 19:25)

Words and Music by
DALE MATHEWS

To the Praise of Your Glorious Grace
(Eph. 1:16)

Words and Music by
ED KEE

164

I'd Rather Have Jesus
(Phil. 3:8)

RHEA F. MILLER

GEORGE BEVERLY SHEA

1. I'd rath - er have Je - sus than sil - ver or gold; I'd
2. He's fair - er than lil - ies of rar - est bloom; He's

rath - er be His than have rich - es un - told;___ I'd
sweet - er than hon - ey from out of the comb;___ He's

rath - er have Je - sus than hous - es or lands. I'd
all that my hun - ger - ing spir - it needs. I'd

rath - er be led by His nail - pierced hand Than to
rath - er have Je - sus and___ let Him lead

be the king___ of a vast___ do - main Or be

It Is Well with My Soul
(Ps. 103:2)

HORATIO G. SPAFFORD

PHILIP P. BLISS

roll; What-ev-er my lot, Thou hast taught me to
whole, Is nailed to the cross and I bear it no
scroll, The trump shall re-sound and the Lord shall de-

say, "It is well, it is well with my
more, Praise the Lord, praise the Lord, O my
scend, "E-ven so"– it is well with my

soul." It is well___ with my soul,___
soul! (It is well)   (with my
soul.

soul,) It is well, it__ is well with my soul.

Sweet Hour of Prayer
(Acts 3:1)

WILLIAM W. WALFORD

WILLIAM B. BRADBURY

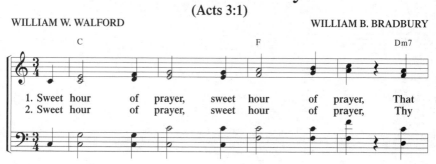

1. Sweet hour of prayer, sweet hour of prayer, That
2. Sweet hour of prayer, sweet hour of prayer, Thy

168

Holy, Holy
(Rev. 4:8b)

Words and Music by
JIMMY OWENS

People Need the Lord
(Matt. 9:35-37)

Words and Music by
GREG NELSON and PHILL McHUGH

Peo-ple need the Lord, peo-ple need the Lord;

At the end of bro-ken dreams, He's the o-pen door.
When will we

re-al-ize that peo-ple need the Lord?

Garment of Praise
(Isa. 61:3)

Words and Music by
DAVID INGLES

Put on the gar-ment of praise for the spir-it of heav-i-ness;

I Love You with the Love of the Lord

(I Peter 1:22)

Words and Music by
JAMES M. GILBERT

Oh, I love you with the love of the Lord.

Yes, I love you with the love of the

Lord. I can see in

you the glo - ry of my King, and I

love you with the love of the Lord.

The Bond of Love
(II John 3:14)

Words and Music by
OTIS SKILLINGS

1. Love through Christ has brought us to-geth - er, Melt - ing our hearts as
2. Now, dear Lord, we join in__ wor - ship; Thank You for all You've

one. By God's Spir - it we are u - nit - ed,
done. Thank You for this love You__ gave__ us;

One through His bless - ed Son. We are one in the bond of
Thank You for mak-ing us one.

love. We are one in the bond of love.__ We have

joined our spir-its with the Spir - it of God; We are one in the bond of love.

Hosanna
(Matt. 21:9)

Words and Music by
CARL TUTTLE

1. Ho - san - na, ho - san - na, Ho - san - na in the high - est;
2. Glo - ry, glo - ry, Glo - ry to the King of Kings;

Ho - san - na, ho - san - na, Ho - san - na in the high - est.
Glo - ry, glo - ry, Glo - ry to the King of Kings.

Lord, we lift up Your name,

With hearts full of praise; Be ex - alt - ed, O

Lord my God, Ho - san - na in the high - est.

Healer
(Ex. 15:26)

Words and Music by
PARRISH PAUL

Jesus, Lord to Me
(Phil. 2:11)

Words and Music by
GARY McSPADDEN and GREG NELSON

Je - sus, Je - sus, Lord to _ me;

Mas - ter, Sav - ior, Prince of _ Peace!

Rul - er _ of my heart to - day,

Je - sus, Lord to me.

He Who Began a Good Work in You

(Phil. 1:6)

Words and Music by
JON MOHR

He who be-gan a good work in you,

He who be-gan a good work in you

will be faith - ful to com-plete it,

He'll be faith - ful to com-plete it; He who start-

ed the work will be faith - ful to com-plete it in you.

Something Beautiful
(Luke 15:24)

Words by
GLORIA GAITHER

Music by
WILLIAM J. GAITHER

O How Thankful I Am
(Ps. 100:4)

Words and Music by
TERRY BUTLER

Earnestly I Seek Your Face
(Ps. 105:4)

Words and Music by
TERRY BUTLER

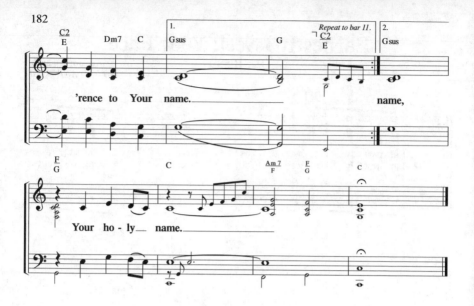

'rence to Your name. name,

Your ho - ly name.

Holy Child
(Isa. 9:6-7)

Words and Music by
DON and LORIE MARSH

Ho - ly Child, we look for Your com-ing, Ho - ly

Child, Your com-ing brings peace. Light to our dark - ness,

joy to our sad - ness, Ho - ly Child, Your com-ing brings peace.

I Stand in Awe
(Ps. 33:8)

Words and Music by
MARK ALTROGGE

You are beau-ti-ful be-yond de-scrip-tion, too mar-vel-ous for words, Too won-der-ful for com-pre-hen-sion, like noth-ing ev-er seen or heard. Who can grasp Your in-fi-nite wis-dom? Who can fath-om the depth of Your love? You are beau-ti-ful be-yond de-scrip-tion, Maj-es-

ty en-throned a-bove. And I stand, I stand in awe of You;___ I

stand, I stand in awe of You.___ Ho-ly God, to Whom all

praise is due, I stand in awe of You! I You!

Psalm
(Ps. 51:10,11)

Words and Music by
BRET PEMELTON

Lord, change my life;___ make my heart sing for___ You.

Lord, may my life___ be a sweet song for You. You.___

The Solid Rock
(Matt. 7:24)

EDWARD MOTE

WILLIAM B. BRADBURY

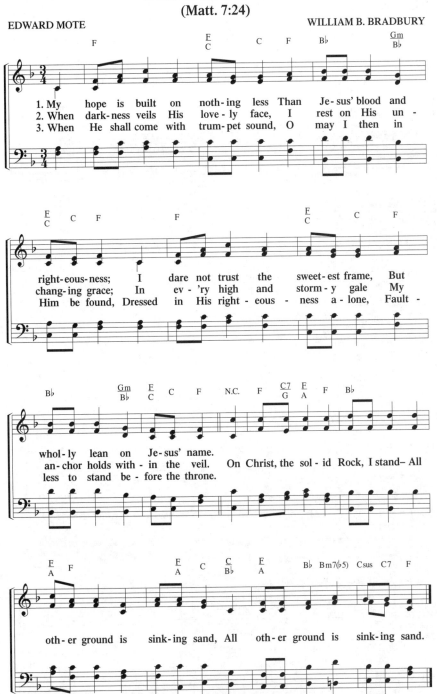

1. My hope is built on noth-ing less Than Je-sus' blood and
2. When dark-ness veils His love-ly face, I rest on His un-
3. When He shall come with trum-pet sound, O may I then in

right-eous-ness; I dare not trust the sweet-est frame, But
chang-ing grace; In ev-'ry high and storm-y gale My
Him be found, Dressed in His right-eous-ness a-lone, Fault-

whol-ly lean on Je-sus' name.
an-chor holds with-in the veil. On Christ, the sol-id Rock, I stand– All
less to stand be-fore the throne.

oth-er ground is sink-ing sand, All oth-er ground is sink-ing sand.

Arr. © 1995 New Spring Publishing/ASCAP, a division of Brentwood Music, Inc.,
One Maryland Farms, Brentwood, TN 37027. All rights reserved. Unauthorized duplication prohibited.

Isn't He?
(Ps. 50:2)

Words and Music by
JOHN WIMBER

Blessed Be the Lord God Almighty
(Rev. 4:8b)

Words and Music by
SHIRLEY POWELL

The Family of God
(Eph. 3:15)

Words and Music by
WILLIAM J. and GLORIA GAITHER

The Battle Belongs to the Lord
(II Chron. 20:1)

Words and Music by
JAMIE OWENS-COLLINS

1. In heav-en-ly ar-mor we'll en-ter the land.___ The
(2.) pow-er of dark-ness comes in___ like a flood,___ The
(3.) en-e-my press-es in hard,___ do not fear:___

bat-tle be-longs___ to the Lord.___ No weap-on that's fash-ioned a-gainst___
He's raised up a stand-ard, the pow'r___
Take cour-age my friend,___ your re-demp-

___ us will stand.___ The bat-tle be-longs___ to the Lord.___ And we sing___
___ of His blood;___
tion is near;___

glo-ry, hon-or, pow-er and strength___ to the Lord.___

___ We sing___ glo-ry, hon-or,

Rock of Ages
(I Cor. 10:4)

AUGUSTUS M. TOPLADY

THOMAS HASTINGS

Thy Word
(Ps. 119:105)

Words and Music by
AMY GRANT and MICHAEL W. SMITH

Thy_____ Word is a lamp un-to___ my feet and a

light un-to my path. path.

When I feel_ a-fraid, think I've lost_ my way, still You're there right be-

side___ me. And noth-ing will_ I fear as_ long as You_ are near;

Please be near me to the end._____

The Trees of the Field
(Isa. 55:12)

Based on Is. 55:12

Words and Music by
STEFFI KAREN RUBIN and STUART DAUERMAN

trees of the field will clap their hands;____ The trees of the

field will clap their hands____ while You go out with

joy. You shall go joy.____

To God Be the Glory
(Ps. 126:3)

FANNY J. CROSBY

WILLIAM H. DOANE

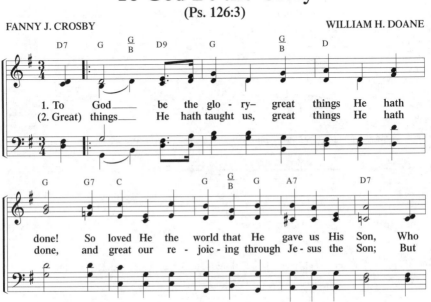

1. To God____ be the glo-ry– great things He hath
(2. Great) things____ He hath taught us, great things He hath

done! So loved He the world that He gave us His Son, Who
done, and great our re-joic-ing through Je-sus the Son; But

We Bow Down
(Ps. 95:6)

Words and Music by
TWILA PARIS

196

Sing Hallelujah to the Lord
(Rev. 19:1)

Words and Music by
LINDA STASSEN

Amazing Grace
(John 9:25)

JOHN NEWTON

Trad. American Melody

He Lives

(Rev. 1:18)

Words and Music by
ALFRED H. ACKLEY

part!_____ You ask me how I

know He lives? He lives with - in my

1. heart._____ *Repeat to bar 1.* 2. Re - heart._____

We Are an Offering
(Rom. 12:1)

Words and Music by
DWIGHT LILES

We lift our voic - es, we lift our hands, We lift our
Lord, use our voic - es, Lord, use our hands; Lord, use our

lives up to You— we are an of - fer-ing;_____ Lord, use our
lives— they are Yours; we are an

Soon and Very Soon
(Rev. 22:20)

Words and Music by
ANDRAÉ CROUCH

1. Soon and ver-y soon___ we are goin' to see the King.___
2. No more cry-in' there,___ we are goin' to see the King.___
3. No more dy-in' there,___ we are goin' to see the King.___
4. Soon and ver-y soon___ we are goin' to see the King.___

Soon and ver-y soon___ we are goin' to see the King.___
No more cry-in' there,___ we are goin' to see the King.___
No more dy-in' there,___ we are goin' to see the King.___
Soon and ver-y soon___ we are goin' to see the King.___

Soon and ver-y soon___ we are goin' to see the King.___ Hal-le-
No more cry-in' there,___ we are goin' to see the King.___
No more dy-in' there,___ we are goin' to see the King.___
Soon and ver-y soon___ we are goin' to see the King.___

lu - jah, hal-le-lu - jah,___ we're goin' to see the King!

Hal - le-lu -

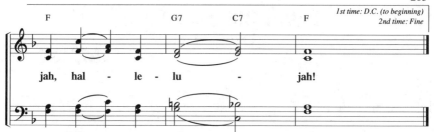

1st time: D.C. (to beginning)
2nd time: Fine

jah, hal - le - lu - jah!

When I Survey the Wondrous Cross
(John 19:37)

ISAAC WATTS

Based on Gregorian Chant;
arr. by LOWELL MASON

1. When I sur - vey the won - drous cross
2. For - bid it, Lord, that I should boast,
3. Were the whole realm of na - ture mine,

On which the Prince of glo - ry died,
Save in the death of Christ, my God;
That were a pres - ent far too small:

My rich - est gain I count but loss,
All the vain things that charm me most–
Love so a - maz - ing, so di - vine,

And pour con - tempt on all my pride.
I sac - ri - fice them to His blood.
De - mands my soul, my life, my all.

I Will Bless the Lord
(Ps. 145:8-10)

Words and Music by
FRANK HERNANDEZ

I will bless the Lord and give Him glo - ry.— Oh, I will bless— His name and give Him glo - ry. The Lord is gra-cious— and— mer-ci-ful, great in kind-ness and good to all. The Lord is right-eous— in— all His ways. Bless the Lord and give Him praise.—

Fine

D.C. al Fine
(to beginning)

Savior, Like a Shepherd Lead Us

(John 10:3)

attr. to DOROTHY A. THRUPP

WILLIAM B. BRADBURY

1. Sav-ior, like a shep-herd lead us, Much we need Thy ten-der care; In Thy pleas-ant pas-tures feed us, For our use Thy folds pre-pare: Bless-ed Je-sus, bless-ed Je-sus, Thou hast bought us, Thine we are; Bless-ed Je-sus, bless-ed Je-sus, Thou hast bought us, Thine we are.

2. Ear-ly let us seek Thy fa-vor; Ear-ly let us do Thy will; Bless-ed Lord and on-ly Sav-ior, With Thy love our bos-oms fill: Bless-ed Je-sus, bless-ed Je-sus, Thou hast loved us, love us still; Bless-ed Je-sus, bless-ed Je-sus, Thou hast loved us, love us still.

Victory in Jesus
(I Cor. 15:57)

Words and Music by
EUGENE M. BARTLETT, Sr.

1. I heard an old, old sto - ry, how a Sav - ior came from glo - ry, How He gave His life on Cal - va - ry to save a wretch like me: I heard a - bout His groan - ing, of His pre - cious blood's a - ton - ing, Then I re - pent - ed of my sins and won the vic - to -

2. I heard a - bout a man - sion He has built for me in glo - ry, And I heard a - bout the streets of gold be - yond the crys - tal sea; A - bout the an - gels sing - ing and the old re - demp - tion sto - ry, And some sweet day I'll sing up there the song of vic - to -

Guide Me, O Thou Great Jehovah

(Isa. 58:11)

WILLIAM WILLIAMS; translated by
PETER WILLIAMS and WILLIAM WILLIAMS

JOHN HUGHES

1. Guide me, O Thou great Je-ho-vah, Pil-grim through this bar-ren land; I am weak, but Thou art might-y; Hold me with Thy pow'r-ful hand; Bread of heav-en, Bread of heav-en, Feed me till I want no more, Feed me till I want no more.

2. When I tread the verge of Jor-dan, Bid my anx-ious fears sub-side; Bear me thro' the swell-ing cur-rent, Land me safe on Ca-naan's side; Songs of prais-es, songs of prais-es I will ev-er give to Thee, I will ev-er give to Thee.

I Must Tell Jesus
(Heb. 2:18)

Words and Music by
ELISHA A. HOFFMAN

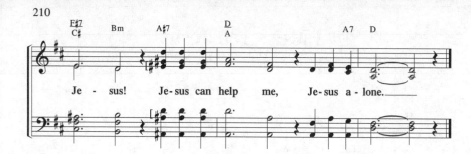

Je - sus! Je - sus can help me, Je - sus a - lone.

He Is Our God
(Ps. 95:7)

Words and Music by
DALE MATHEWS

He is our God and we have trust - ed Him;

He is our God and He has saved

us. He is the Lord, re - joice in His sal - va - tion;

He is our God, He is our God.

The Church's One Foundation

(Isa. 28:16)

SAMUEL J. STONE

SAMUEL S. WESLEY

1. The church-'s one foun - da - tion Is Je - sus Christ her Lord; She is His new cre - a - tion By wa - ter and the Word: From heav'n He came and sought her to be His ho - ly bride; With His own blood He bought her, And for her life He died.

2. E - lect from ev - 'ry na - tion, Yet one o'er all the earth, Her char - ter of sal - va - tion One Lord, one faith, one birth; One ho - ly name she bless - es, Par - takes one ho - ly food, And to one hope she press - es, With ev - 'ry grace en - dued.

3. Yet she on earth hath un - ion With God the Three in One, And mys - tic sweet com - mun - ion With those whose rest is won: O hap - py ones and ho - ly! Lord, give us grace that we, Like them, the meek and low - ly, On high may dwell with Thee.

Christ the Lord Is Risen Today
(I Cor. 15:55)

CHARLES WESLEY

from *Lyra Davidica*, London, 1708

1. Christ the Lord is ris'n to-day,__ Al - le - lu - ia!
2. Lives a - gain our glo - rious King,__ Al - le - lu - ia!
3. Love's re - deem - ing work is done,__ Al - le - lu - ia!
4. Soar we now where Christ has led, Al - le - lu - ia!

Sons of men and an - gels say:__ Al - le - lu - ia!
Where, O death, is now thy sting?__ Al - le - lu - ia!
Fought the fight, the bat - tle won,__ Al - le - lu - ia!
Fol - l'wing our ex - alt - ed Head, Al - le - lu - ia!

Raise your joys and__ tri - umphs high, Al - le - lu - ia!
Dy - ing once He__ all doth save, Al - le - lu - ia!
Death in vain for - bids Him rise, Al - le - lu - ia!
Made like Him, like__ Him we rise, Al - le - lu - ia!

Sing,__ ye heav'ns, and__ earth re - ply:__ Al - le - lu - ia!
Where thy vic - to - ry, O grave?__ Al - le - lu - ia!
Christ has o - pened Par - a - dise,__ Al - le - lu - ia!
Ours the cross, the grave, the skies,__ Al - le - lu - ia!

Crown Him with Many Crowns

(Rev. 19:12)

MATTHEW BRIDES
GODFREY THRING

GEORGE J. ELVEY

1. Crown Him with man - y crowns, The lamb up - on His throne: Hark! how the heav'n - ly an - them drowns All mu - sic but its own! A - wake, my soul, and sing Of Him who died for thee, And hail Him as thy match - less King Thru all e - ter - ni - ty.

2. Crown Him the Lord of life: Who tri - umphed o'er the grave, Who rose vic - to - rious to the strife For those He came to save. His glo - ries now we sing, Who died and rose on high, Who died e - ter - nal life to bring And lives that death may die.

3. Crown Him the Lord of heav'n: One with the Fa - ther known, One with the Spir - it thru Him giv'n From yon - der glo - rious throne. To Thee be end - less praise, For Thou for us hast died; Be Thou, O Lord, thru end - less days A - dored and mag - ni - fied.

214

Come, Thou Fount of Every Blessing

(Prov. 10:22)

ROBERT ROBINSON;
adapted by MARGARET CLARKSON

Trad. American Melody

1. Come, Thou Fount of ev-ery bless-ing, Tune my heart to sing Thy grace; Streams of mer-cy, nev-er ceas-ing, Call for songs of loud-est praise. Teach me some me-lo-dious son-net, Sung by flam-ing tongues a-bove; Praise His name— I'm fixed up-on it— Name of God's re-deem-ing love.

2. O to grace how great a debt-or Dai-ly I'm con-strained to be! Let Thy good-ness, like a fet-ter, Bind my wan-dering heart to Thee: Prone to— wan-der, Lord, I feel— it, Prone to— leave the God I love; Here's my heart, O take and seal it; Seal it for Thy courts a-bove.

At the Cross
(I Cor. 1:18)

ISAAC WATTS;
RALPH E. HUDSON, Refrain

RALPH E. HUDSON

1. A — las! and did my Sav — ior bleed? And did my Sov-'reign
2. But drops of grief can ne'er re — pay The debt of love I

die? Would He de — vote that Sa — cred head for sin — ners such as
owe: Here, Lord, I give my — self a — way-'Tis all that I can

I!
do! At the cross, at the cross where I first— saw the light And the

bur — den of my heart rolled a — way— It was there by— faith I re-

ceived my— sight, And now I am hap — py all the day!

Our Great Savior
(Titus 2:13-14)

J. WILBUR CHAPMAN

ROWLAND H. PRICHARD

1. Je - sus! what a Friend for sin - ners!
2. Je - sus! what a Strength in weak - ness!
3. Je - sus! I do now re - ceive Him,

Je - sus! Lov - er of my soul;
Let me hide my - self in Him;
More than all in Him I find;

Friends may fail me, foes as - sail me,
Tempt - ed, tried, and some - times fail - ing,
He hath grant - ed me for - give - ness,

He, my Sav - ior, makes me whole.
He, my Strength, my vic - t'ry wins.
I am His, and He is mine.

Hal - le - lu - jah! what a Sav - ior!

Hal - le - lu - jah! what a Friend!

Sav - ing, help - ing, keep - ing, lov - ing,

He is with me to the end.

Hiding in Thee
(Ps. 61:2)

WILLIAM O. CUSHING

IRA D. SANKEY

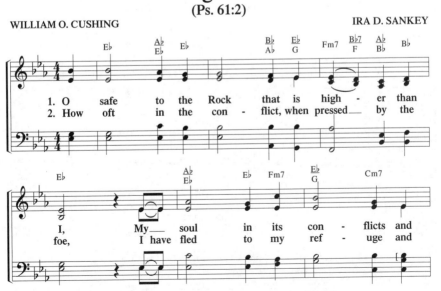

1. O safe to the Rock that is high - er than
2. How oft in the con - flict, when pressed by the

I, My soul in its con - flicts and
foe, I have fled to my ref - uge and

218

Abide with Me
(Duet. 31:6)

HENRY F. LYTE

WILLIAM H. MONK

1. A - bide with me! Fast falls the e - ven - tide.
2. I need Thy pres - ence ev - 'ry pass - ing hour.
3. I fear no foe, with Thee at hand to bless;

The dark - ness deep - ens; Lord, with me a -
What but Thy grace can foil the tempt - er's
Ills have no weight, and tears no bit - ter -

bide! When oth - er help - ers
pow'r? Who, like Thy - self, my
ness. Where is death's sting? Where,

fail and com - forts flee, Help of the
guide and stay can be? Thro' clouds and
grave, thy vic - to - ry? I tri - umph

help - less, Oh, a - bide with me!
sun - shine, Oh, a - bide with me!
still if Thou a - bide with me!

Beneath the Cross of Jesus
(John 19:25)

ELIZABETH C. CLEPHANE

FREDERICK C. MAKER

1. Be - neath the cross of Je - sus I fain would take my stand– The shad - ow of a might - y Rock With - in a wea - ry land;____ A home with - in the wil - der - ness, A rest____ up - on the way,____ From the burn - ing of the noon- tide heat, And the bur - den of the day.

2. I take, O cross, thy shad - ow For my a - bid - ing place; I ask no oth - er sun - shine than The sun - shine of His face;____ Con - tent to let the world go____ by, To know____ no gain nor loss,____ My____ sin - ful self my on - ly shame, My____ glo - ry all the cross.

O Worship the King

(Ps. 104:1)

ROBERT GRANT

Attr. to JOHANN MICHAEL HAYDN;
arr. by WILLIAM GARDINER, 1815

1. O wor - ship the King, all glo - rious a -
bove, And grate - ful - ly sing His
won - der - ful love; Our Shield and De -
fend - er, the An - cient of Days, Pa -
vil - ioned in splen - dor, and gird - ed with praise.

2. O tell of His might, O sing of His
grace, Whose robe is the light, whose
can - o - py space! His char - iots of
wrath the deep thun - der - clouds form, And
dark is His path on the wings of the storm.

3. Frail chil - dren of dust, and fee - ble as
frail, In Thee do we trust, nor
find Thee to fail: Thy mer - cies how
ten - der, how firm to the end, Our
Mak - er, De - fend - er, Re - deem - er, and Friend.

No One Understands Like Jesus

(Heb. 4:15)

Words and Music by
JOHN W. PETERSON

1. No one un-der-stands like Je-sus, He's a friend be-yond com-
2. No one un-der-stands like Je-sus, When you fal-ter on the

pare; Meet Him at the throne of mer-cy,_____
way; Tho' you fail Him, sad-ly fail Him,_____

He is wait-ing for you there.
He will par-don you to-day.

No one un-der-stands like

Je-sus, When the days are dark and grim;_____ No one is so near, so

dear as Je-sus, Cast your ev-'ry care on Him._____

This Is My Father's World
(Ps. 50:12)

MALTBIE D. BABCOCK

FRANKLIN L. SHEPPARD

1. This is my Fa-ther's world, And to my lis-t'ning ears All na-ture sings, and round me rings The mu-sic of the spheres. This is my Fa-ther's world: I rest me in the thought Of rocks and trees, of skies and seas— His hand the won-ders wrought.

2. This is my Fa-ther's world, O let me ne'er for-get That though the wrong seems oft so strong, God is the Rul-er yet. This is my Fa-ther's world: The bat-tle is not done; Je-sus who died shall be sat-is-fied, And earth and heav'n be one.

224

To Your Name
(Ps. 13:5-6)

Words and Music by
ED CANTRELL

I will lift my voice un-to Your name, I will sing though no one join my song; When the pain and tri-als come my way, I will sing, I will sing to Your name.

Jesus Paid It All
(I Cor. 6:19-20)

ELVINA M. HALL

JOHN T. GRAPE

Hail, Holy King
(Rev. 4)

Words and Music by
WES SWIGER, ALAN CRAIG, BEV GIBBONS,
JAMES BURTCH and ED KEE

Hail, Ho-ly King, wor - ship we bring; Prais - es we sing, hail, Ho - ly King. Won - der - ful Coun - sel - or,

King of__ all king - doms,__ now and__ for - ev - er__ the same;__ Lord, we__ a - dore You__ and bow - ing__ be - fore You,__ we praise and lift Your ho - ly name.__

D.C. al Fine
(Repeat to beginning)

And Can It Be?
(Eph. 2:7)

CHARLES WESLEY   THOMAS CAMPBELL

1. And can it be that I__ should__ gain An
2. He left His Fa - ther's throne__ a - bove, So
3. No con - dem - na - tion now__ I__ dread: Je -

Almighty
(Rev. 11:17)

Words and Music by
WAYNE WATSON

A Mighty Fortress Is Our God

(Ps. 46:7)

MARTIN LUTHER

1. A might - y for - tress is our God,
2. Did we in our own strength con - fide,
3. And tho' this world, with dev - ils filled,
4. That word a - bove all earth - ly pow'rs,

A bul - wark nev - er fail - ing; Our help - er He a -
Our striv - ing would be los - ing, Were not the right man
Should threat - en to un - do us, We will not fear, for
No thanks to them, a - bid - eth; The Spir - it and the

mid the flood Of mor - tal ills pre -
on our side, The man of God's own
God hath willed His truth to tri - umph
gifts are ours Through Him who with us

vail - ing. For still our an - cient
choos - ing. Dost ask who that may
through us. The prince of dark - ness
sid - eth. Let goods and kin - dred

G   C   G7sus/D   C/E   F   E7   Am   E/G#

foe   Doth seek_ to work_ us woe–   His
be?   Christ Je - sus, it_ is He–   Lord
grim,   We trem - ble not_ for him–   His
go,   This mor - tal life_ al - so–   The

Am   E/B   Am/C   D   G   F   C   A/C#   Dm

craft and pow'r are_ great,   And, armed with_ cru - el
Sab - a - oth His name,   From age to_ age the
rage we can en - dure,   For, lo, his_ doom is
bod - y they may_ kill;   God's truth a - bid - eth

E   Am   Em/G   F   C/E   A   Dm   G   C

hate,   On earth is not is   e -   qual.
same,   And He must win the bat -   tle.
sure: One lit - tle word shall fell_   him.
still: His king - dom is for - ev -   er.

Fill My Cup, Lord
(John 4:14)

Words and Music by
RICHARD BLANCHARD

Bb   B°7   F7/C   F

1. Like the wo - man at the well, I was seek - ing_____   For
2. So, my bro - ther, if the things this world gave you_____   Leave

232

He Giveth More Grace
(James 4:6)

ANNIE JOHNSON FLINT

HUBERT MITCHELL

love has no lim- it; His grace has no meas- ure; His

pow'r has no boun- da- ry known un- to men.___ For

out of His in- fi- nite rich- es in Je- sus, He

giv- eth, and giv- eth, and giv- eth a- gain!

My Hope Is in the Lord
(Ps. 62:5-8; 130)

Words and Music by
NANCY GORDON

My hope is in the Lord,___ my hope is in the Lord;___ He

Lamb of God
(John 1:29)

Words by
CLAY CLARKSON

Music by
ED KEE

Lamb of God, slain for all, stained by sin from A - dam's fall; Lamb of God, raised to be praised by all re - deemed in Thee; Lamb of God, I wor - ship Thee.

May the Lord Be with You
(Num. 6:24-26)

Words and Music by
STEVE JONES

238

Heaven Came Down
(Gal. 6:15)

Words and Music by
JOHN W. PETERSON

1. O what a won-der-ful, won-der-ful day—
2. Now I've a hope that will sure-ly en-dure

Day I will nev-er for-get; After I'd wan-dered in
Af-ter the pass-ing of time; I have a fu-ture in

dark-ness a-way, Je-sus my Sav-ior I met.
heav-en for sure, There in those man-sions sub-lime.

O what a ten-der, com-pas-sion-ate friend—
And it's be-cause of that won-der-ful day

He met the need of my heart; Shad-ows dis-pel-ling, With
When at the cross I be-lieved; Rich-es e-ter-nal and

joy I am tell-ing, He made all the dark-ness de-part!
bless-ings su-per-nal, From His pre-cious hand I re-ceived.

Heav-en came down and glo-ry filled my soul,____ (filled my

When at the cross the Sav-ior made me

____ soul,)

whole;____ (made me whole;)____ My sins were washed a-

way____ And my night was turned to day—____

Heav-en came down and glo-ry filled my soul!____ (filled my soul!)

What a Mighty God We Serve
(Ps. 145:4)

AUTHOR UNKNOWN

What a might-y God we serve,

What a might-y God we serve;

An-gels bow be-fore Him, Heav-en and earth a-

dore Him. *suggested intro* What a might-y God we

serve.

No Other God
(I Sam. 2:2)

Words and Music by
TROY and GENIE NILSON

Let the Redeemed
(Of the Lord Say So)
(Ps. 71:23)

Words and Music by
WARD ELLIS

How Kind and Gracious Is the Lord
(Ps. 103:8)

Words and Music by
ED KEE

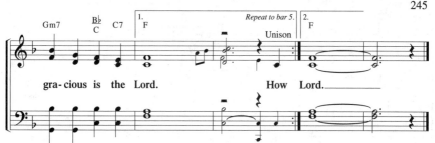

gra-cious is the Lord.　　How　Lord.

People of God
(I Pet. 2:9)

Words and Music by
WAYNE WATSON

1. With our lips let us sing one con- fes -
2. Hear us, O spir- its of dark -

sion, with our hearts hold to one truth a - lone;
ness, so you will know where we stand;

For He has e - rased our trans- gres -
We are His ser- vants, pur - chased with

sion, claimed us and called us His own,
scars, bought by the blood of the Lamb, the

I Rise in Christ
(Rom. 6:4)

Words and Music by
STEVE LYNAM

1. As a sac-ri-fi-cial Lamb,___ You be-came what You were not That now I might be who I am___ in Christ, the right-eous-ness___ of God. I rise, I___ rise in Christ,___ I rise___ in Christ.___ I rise,___ I rise

2. Ho-ly Spir-it, look with-in,___ pour Your___ life and joy in me; Fill ev-'ry space where sin has___ been,___ I die a-gain on bend-ed knee. I rise, I___ rise in Christ,___ I rise___ in Christ.___ You

Lamb of God
(John 1:29)

Words and Music by
TWILA PARIS

Mighty Is Your Name
(Jer. 10:6)

Words and Music by
MARK HAUTH

We Are His Praise
(Heb. 13:15)

Words and Music by
KIRK and DEBY DEARMAN

We are His praise, we are His praise, As we live right-eous-ly in all our ways. We are His praise, we are His praise; As we live right-eous-ly, we are His praise!

1. Sing with your
2. I want to

heart,_____ sing with___ your voice,_____
live_____ what I___ pro - fess;_____

Sing a_____ new song to___ the Lord and___ re -
I will___ not set - tle___ for an - y - thing

joice!_____ Live what you sing_____
less!_____ Help me__ to walk_____

all of___ your days;_____ Let your__ whole
in all___ Your ways;_____ Lord, make__ my

life be__ a love song__ of praise!
life be__ a love song__ of praise!

D.C.
(Repeat to beginning)

By Your Hand
(I Chron. 29:1)

Words and Music by
ED KEE

1. We've been blessed be-yond all meas-ure by the rich-es of Your grace,_____ for Your hand-i-work_____ is seen through-out our land._____

2. By Your hand You have pro-vid-ed, by Your hand our lives are blessed,_____ and with con-fi-dence_____ and trust in You we stand._____

And what-ev-er earth-ly treas-ure we may cher-ish or em-

For our hearts are un-di-vid-ed, know-ing all that we pos-

256

bless-ings we are giv-en by Your hand.

Love Lifted Me
(I John 4:10)

JAMES ROWE   HOWARD E. SMITH

1. I was sink - ing deep in sin, Far from the peace - ful
2. All my heart to Him I give, Ev - er to Him I'll
3. Souls in dan - ger, look a - bove, Je - sus com - plete - ly

shore,_____ Ver - y deep - ly stained with - in,
cling,_____ In His bless - ed pres - ence live,
saves;_____ He will lift you by His love

Sink-ing to rise no more;_____ But the Mas - ter
Ev - er His prais - es sing;_____ Love so might - y
Out of the an - gry waves;_____ He's the Mas - ter

of the sea Heard my des - pair - ing cry,_____
and so true Mer - its my soul's best songs;_____
of the sea, Bil - lows His will o - bey;_____

258

Key, Tempo & Meter Index

Scripture Reference Index

262

New Testament

Topical Index

Hymns

Jesus, the Son

Joy

Name of Jesus

Praise

Index of Titles & First Lines